AF365574

Colección: Libros de inglés para Infantil y Primaria

Cuentos y poesías en inglés para infantil 4 años

THE LITTLE SHEEP WENT TO SCHOOL (SCHOOL)

EVERYBODY HELPS AT HOME (FAMILY)

CHARLIE HAS GOT A NEW TOY
(CHISTMAS AND TOYS)

THE SMALL MAGGOT IS DANCING
(BODY AND WINTER)

THE DRAGON HAS GOT A COLD (CLOTHES)

LET'S GO TO THE RESTAURANT (FOOD)

HENS SHARE EASTER EGGS
(SPRING AND EASTER)

A VERY NAUGHTY SNAKE (ANIMALS)

I WANT AN ICE CREAM (SUMMER)

A TREE WITHOUT A NAME
(EARTH DAY / "DÍA DEL ÁRBOL")

THE SUN AND THE MOON WANTED TO GET MARRIED
(MOTHER'S DAY)

DAD! THERE'S A CHOCOLATE CAKE FOR YOU!
(FATHER'S DAY)

Copyright © Pilar Bellés Pitarch, 2014
1ª edición: agosto 2014
ISBN 978-84-617-1333-2
Depósito Legal: CS-268-2014

Pilar Bellés Pitarch (1964). Es licenciada en Filología Inglesa y profesora de inglés. Hace años que se dedica a investigar sobre las posibilidades del cuento para desarrollar la creatividad y trabajar valores. También cuenta con investigaciones sobre métodos para aprender inglés.

Estos son los cuentos y poesías que usa en sus clases de inglés. Cada cuento tiene sus imágenes en color y su poema. A los niños de esta edad les gusta recitar poemas en lengua extranjera y así, mientras escuchan el cuento en inglés interactúan y usan la lengua.

Son de gran utilidad tanto para los profesores o profesoras de inglés como para los padres y madres que quieran mejorar el nivel de inglés de sus hijos o hijas.

Pilar Bellés cuenta además con numerosas publicaciones en cuento, novela y poesía.

Publicaciones sobre cuentos plurilingües y valores en el campo de la enseñanza:

•"Telling a tale / Contemos un cuento / Contem un conte" (adaptados a los centros de interés de educación infantil).

• "Cuentos plurilingües para trabajar valores y para días especiales" (día del árbol, día de la paz, Halloween…)

•"¿Cómo hacer alumnos creativos?" (cuentos plurilingües para desarrollar la creatividad y, a la vez, trabajar valores para todas las edades).

• "No dejes que crezca sin la magia de los cuentos… según lo que quieras transmitir, elige un cuento y… cuéntaselo" (alternativa a los cuentos tradicionales).

Métodos para aprender inglés a través de la literatura:

•"Els iaios, la natura i l'amor / Los abuelos, la naturaleza y el amor / Grandparents, Love and Nature" (método de las historias plurilingües).

•"Federico y su duende / Frederick and his Goblin" (método de las historias bilingües).

Novela:

•"El diario mágico" (contra la violencia de género). Ediciones Carena.

•"Somos víctimas de una sociedad machista y cruel" (contra el machismo y la desigualdad). Ediciones Grup Lobher.

•"El mensaje" (contra el acoso y la manipulación). Ediciones Carena.

•"La rosa deshojada" (contra la violencia de género) de Pilar Bellés y Maribel Rueda. JNQ Ediciones.

•"Triunfar en tiempos difíciles" con el método de los relatos interrelacionados. JNQ Ediciones.

."Reunión de colegas" (se nos manipula sin que nos demos cuenta…). Editorial Lulu.

    Biografía:
. "Toda una vida: memorias y anécdotas de Mel y Xispa". De Manuel Falcó García (Xispa) y Pilar Bellés Pitarch. Editorial viveLibro.

. Teatro: "Engaño perfecto". Editorial Lulu.

. Poesía: "Curvas en el camino". Ediciones Carena.

. Ensayo: "Educar en valores actuales a través de la literatura y otros ensayos". Editorial Lulu.

THE LITLE SHEEP WENT TO SCHOOL
(SCHOOL)

ONCE UPON A TIME THERE WAS A LITTLE SHEEP THAT WENT TO SCHOOL. SHE DIDN'T TALK OR KNOW THE NAMES OF EVERYTHING. SHE WANTED EDUCATION AND KNOWLEDGE.
'HELLO!' SAID THE HORSE. HE NEIGHED.
'HELLO!' SAID THE DOG. HE BARKED 'WOOF! WOOF!'
 'BAA!' SAID THE LITTLE SHEEP.
THE HORSE AND THE DOG BECAME SAD, VERY SAD.

LITTLE SHEEP, LITTLE SHEEP,
HELLO, HELLO, HELLO,
NO, NO, NO…
SAD, SAD, SAD.

DURING THE NEXT DAYS THE SHEEP BEGAN TO LEARN NEW WORDS:
'LOOK, LITTLE SHEEP, THIS IS A PENCIL,' SAID THE TEACHER.
'THIS IS A PENCIL,' REPEATED THE HORSE. HE NEIGHED.
'THIS IS A PENCIL,' REPEATED THE DOG. HE BARKED 'WOOF! WOOF!'
'A PENCIL!' SAID THE SHEEP.
EVERYBODY BECAME HAPPY AND CLAPPED HIS HANDS.

A PENCIL, A PENCIL,
YES, YES, YES…
HAPPY, HAPPY, HAPPY,
CLAP, CLAP, CLAP.

'LOOK, LITTLE SHEEP, THIS IS A RUBBER,' SAID THE TEACHER.

'THIS IS A RUBBER,' REPEATED THE HORSE. HE NEIGHED.
'THIS IS A RUBBER,' REPEATED THE DOG. HE BARKED 'WOOF! WOOF!'
'A RUBBER!' SAID THE SHEEP.
EVERYBODY SMILED AND CLAPPED HIS HANDS.

A RUBBER, A RUBBER,
YES, YES, YES…
HAPPY, HAPPY, HAPPY,
CLAP, CLAP, CLAP.

'LOOK, LITTLE SHEEP, 'THESE ARE PENCILS' THESE ARE CRAYONS', 'THIS IS GLUE', 'THESE ARE SCISSORS' , 'THESE ARE PAPERS', 'THIS IS A BOOK', 'THIS IS A PUZZLE', THESE ARE PAINTS' AND 'THIS IS PLASTICINE'
SO, THY REPEATED THE WORDS UNTIL THE LITTLE SHEEP COULD LEARN THEM.

PENCILS, CRAYONS, GLUE,
SCISSORS, PAPERS, BOOK,
PUZLE, PAINTS,
AND PLASTICINE.

PENCILS   CRAYONS   GLUE

SCISSORS   PAPERS   BOOK

PUZZLE   PAINTS   PLASTICINE

ONE DAY THE LITTLE SHEEP LOST HER PENCIL.
'A PENCIL, PLEASE?'
'YES, HERE YOU ARE', SAID ONE STUDENT.
 'THANK YOU,' SAID THE SEEP.
'YOU ARE WELCOME,' SAID THE TEACHER.
OTHER DAYS THE LITTLE SHEEP ASKED FOR EVERYTHING:
RUBBERS, CRAYONS, GLUE...

A PENCIL, PLEASE,
YES, HERE YOU ARE,
THANK YOU,
YOU ARE WELCOME.
A RUBBER, PLEASE,
YES, HERE YOU ARE,
THANK YOU,
YOU ARE WELCOME.

'BYE-BYE,' SAID THE SHEEP. SHE WENT OUT.
BYE-BYE,' SAID THE SHEEP.
BYE-BYE,' SAID THE SHEEP.
AND THE LITTLE SHEEP WAS VERY WELLMANNERED.

EDUCATION, EDUCATION,
YES, YES, YES,
WE ARE HAPPY,
ONE, TWO, THREE..

GOOD BYE TEACHER
GOOD BYE HORSE
GOOD BYE DOG
GOOD BYE LITTLE SHEEP.

THE LITTLE SHEEP WENT TO SCHOOL

LITTLE SHEEP, LITTLE SHEEP,
HELLO, HELLO, HELLO,
NO, NO, NO…
SAD, SAD, SAD.

A PENCIL, A PENCIL,
YES, YES, YES….
HAPPY, HAPPY, HAPPY,
CLAP, CLAP, CLAP.

A RUBBER, A RUBBER
YES, YES, YES…
HAPPY, HAPPY, HAPPY,
CLAP, CLAP, CLAP.

A PENCIL, PLEASE,
YES, HERE YOU ARE,
THANK YOU
YOU ARE WELCOME.

EDUCATION, EDUCATION,
YES, YES, YES,
WE ARE HAPPY,
ONE, TWO, THREE.

GOOD BYE TEACHER,
GOOD BYE HORSE,
GOOD BYE DOG,,
GOOD BYE LITTLE SHEEP.

EVERYBODY HELPS AT HOME
(FAMILY)

IT WAS HOT. THE FAMILY WAS TAKING A NAP AFTER LUNCH.
EVERYBODY WAS SILENT IN ORDER TO SLEEP.
"CAN THEY SLEEP?"
"NO, NO, NO... EVERYBODY IS AWAKE."

MUM, DAD
BROTHER, SISTER
HAPPY, HAPPY,
MY FAMILY IS TOGETHER.

SLEEP, SLEEP
NO, NO, NO.
AWAKE, AWAKE,
YES, YES, YES.

"CAN MUM SLEEP?"
"NO, NO, NO."
MUM WAS IN THE KITCHEN. SHE WANTED TO LISTEN TO MUSIC BUT SHE COULDN'T BECAUSE EVERBODY MUST BE QUIET.

IN THE KITCHEN
MUM IS QUIET
SHE CAN'T SLEEP
SHE CAN'T LISTEN TO MUSIC
OH NO! OH NO!

"CAN DAD SLEEP?"
"NO, NO, NO. DAD WAS IN THE LIVENG-ROOM. HE WANTED TO WATCH TV, BUT HE COULDN'T. EVERYBODY MUST BE QUIET."

IN THE LIVING ROOM
DAD IS QUIET
HE CAN'T SLEEP
HE CAN'T WATCH TV
OH NO! OH NO!

"CAN THE BROTHER AND HIS SISTER SLEEP?"
'NO, NO, NO. THE BROTHER AND HIS SISTER WERE IN THEIR BEDROOM. THEY WANTED TO PLAY WITH THEIR FRIEND BUT THEY COULDN'T. EVERYBODY MUSY BE QUIET."

IN THEIR ROOM
THE BROTHER AND HIS SISTER
ARE PLAYING QUIETLY
ONE, TWO, THREE.

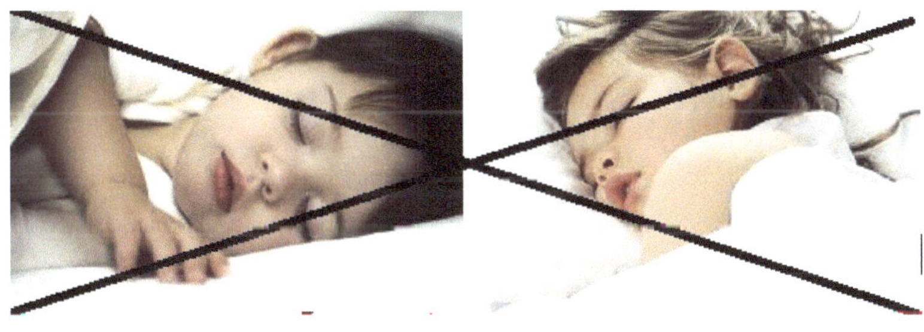

SUDDENLY THE DOORBELL RANG.IT WASTHEIR NEIGHBOUR. SHE WANTED TO LEAVE THEIR CHILDREN BECAUSE SHE MUST GO TO THE DOCTOR. THEY WANTED TO PLAY…
'HURRAY! CAN WE GO TO PLAY, MUM?'
'OK. PLAY IN YOUR BEDROOM. DON'T MAKE NOISE.'

COLLABORATE, COLLABORATE,
YES, YES, YES
PLAY TOGETHER
YES, YES, YES…

FINALLY THE CHILDREN COULD PLAY WITH THEIR FRIENDS IN THEIR BEDROOM UNTIL THEY FELL ASLEEP. MUM COULD LISTEN TO MUSIC AND DAD COULD WATCH TV. EVERYBODY IS HAPPY BECAUSE EVERYBODY COLLABORATED WITH THE OTHERS AT HOME.

COLLABORATE, COLLABORATE,
YES, YES, YES
PLAY TOGETHER
YES, YES, YES…
LISTEN TO MUSIC
YES, YES, YES
WATCH TV
YES, YES, YES.
WE ARE HAPPY
ONE, TWO, THREE.

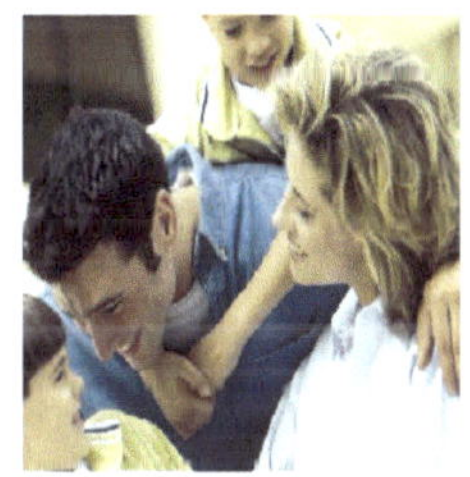

COLLABORATE

MUM, DAD
BROTHER, SISTER
HAPPY, HAPPY,
MY FAMILY IS TOGETHER.

SLEEP, SLEEP
NO, NO, NO.
AWAKE, AWAKE,
YES, YES, YES.

IN THE KITCHEN
MUM IS QUIET
SHE CAN'T SLEEP
SHE CAN'T LISTEN TO MUSIC
OH NO! OH NO!

IN THE LIVING ROOM
DAD IS QUIET
HE CAN'T SLEEP
HE CAN'T LISTEN TO MUSIC
OH NO! OH NO!

IN THEIR ROOM
BROTHER AND SISTER
ARE PLAYING QUIETLY
ONE, TWO, THREE.

COLLABORATE, COLLABORATE,

YES, YES, YES
PLAY TOGETHER
YES, YES, YES…
LISTEN TO MUSIC
YES, YES, YES
WATCH TV
YES, YES, YES.
WE ARE HAPPY
ONE, TWO, THREE.

CHARLIE HAS GOT A NEW TOY
(CHRISTMAS AND TOYS)

ONCE UPON A TIME THERE WAS A SMALL BOY CALLED CHARLIE. HE WAS VERY PROUD OF HIS TOYS. HE HAD LOSTS OF CARS AND A CAR PARKING, A BALL, A DRUM, A KITE, A BALLOON, A TRAIN, A BOAT... BUT HIS FAVOURITE TOY WAS A TEDDY BEAR. THE DAY AFTER CHRISTMAS HOLIDAY, THE TEACHER ASKED STUDENTS TO BRING A TOY TO SCHOOL TO SHARE WITH THEIR PARTNERS.

I'M CHARLIE, A BOY,
DO YOU LIKE MY TOYS?,
A LORRY, A CAR, AND A BALL,
A PARKING, A KITE AND A DRUM
A TRAIN, A BOAT AND A BALLOON.

CHARLIE TOOK HIS TEDDY BEAR, JOHN TOOK HIS TEDDY BEAR, JOHN TOOK HIS LORRY AND JOHN TOOK HIS TRAIN. THEY ARRIVED AT SCHOOL:
'CAN I HAVE YOUR TEDDY BEAR?' ASKED JOHN. 'YOU CAN HAVE MY TOY.'
'NO, NO, NO… IT'S MINE.'
'PLEASE!'
'NO, NO, NO. GO AWAY!'

CHARLIE'S GOT A TEDDY
JOHN'S GOT A LORRY
PAUL'S GOT A TRAIN,
TOYS, TOYS, TOYS.

CHARLIE WAS HAPPY WITH HIS NEW TOY. BUT JOHN WAS SAD.
LATER CHARLIE WAS BORED WITH HIS TOY AND HE WANTED TO CHANGE IT.
'NO, NO, NO' SAID JOHN.
'PLEASE!'
'NO, NO, NO. GO AWAY.'
CHARLIE WAS VERY SAD.
'I AM SORRY,' SAID CHARLIE.
'IT'S OK,' SAID JOHN.

SHARE, SHARE, SHARE
NO, NO, NO
SAD, SAD, SAD…
I AM SORRY!
OK, OK,
SHARE, SHARE,
YES, YES, YES…

'CAN WE PLAY TOGETHER?'
'OK.'
'THANK YOU.'
'YOU ARE WELCOME.'
THEY PLAY TOGETHER AND SHARED OUT THEIR TOYS WITH OTHER STUDENTS. IT WAS AMUSING!

PLAY TOGETHER
YES, YES, YES
YOU ARE HAPPY
ONE, TWO, THREE.

TOYS

I'M CHARLIE, A BOY,
DO YOU LIKE MY TOYS?,
A LORRY, A CAR, AND A BALL,
A PARKING, A KITE AND A DRUM
A TRAIN, A BOAT AND A BALLOON,

CHARLIE'S GOT A TEDDY
JOHN'S GOT A LORRY
PAUL'S GOT A TRAIN,
TOYS, TOYS, TOYS.

SHARE, SHARE, SHARE
NO, NO, NO
SAD, SAD, SAD…

I AM SORRY!
OK, OK,
SHARE, SHARE,
YES, YES, YES…

PLAY TOGETHER
YES, YES, YES
YOU ARE HAPPY
ONE, TWO, THREE.

THE SMALL MAGGOT IS DANCING
(BODY AND WINTER)

IT WAS ELEVEN O'CLOCK AT NIGHT. DAD WAS SLEPING, MUM WAS SLEEPING, BROTHER WAS SLEEPING AND SISTER WAS SLEEPING, BUT THE SMALL MAGGOT WAS DANCING AND DANCING IN FRONT OF THE LIGHT.

ONE, TWO,
WINK YOUR EYE,
WHISTLE WITH YOUR MOUTH.
THREE, FOUR,
SHAKE YOUR HEAD,
NOD YOUR HEAD.
FIVE, SIX,
MOVE YOUR ARMS,
MOVE YOUR LEGS.
SEVEN, EIGHT,
MOVE YOUR BODY,
NINE, TEN,
AND START AGAIN…

'THAT'S ALL FOR TODAY!' SAID MUM.
'JUST A MOMENT, PLEASE, MUM.'
HE DANCED AND DANCED.

ONE, TWO,
WINK YOUR EYE,
WHISTLE WITH YOUR MOUTH.
THREE, FOUR,
SHAKE YOUR HEAD,
NOD YOUR HEAD.
FIVE, SIX,
SHAKE YOUR HEAD,
NOD YOUR HEAD.
FIVE, SIX,
MOVE YOUR ARMS,
MOVE YOUR LEGS.
SEVEN, EIGHT,
MOVE YOUR BODY,
NINE, TEN,
AND START AGAIN…

'LET'S GO,' SAID MUM.
'ONE MOMENT, PLEASE…'
FINALLY HE WENT TO BED.
'WHY WERE YOU DANCING?' ASKED MUM.
'BECAUSE THE LITTLE BOY OF THE HOUSE COULDN'T SLEEP
AND HE NEEDED MY DANCE TO FALL ASLEEP'
'OK,' SAID MUM, 'I'M PROUD OF YOU'
'GOOD NIGHT.'

MUM IS HAPPY
ONE TWO THREE,
YOU SLEEP HAPPILY
ONE, TWO, THREE.

MOVE YOUR BODY

ONE, TWO,
WINK ONE EYE,
WHISTLE YOUR MOUTH.
THREE, FOUR,
SHAKE YOUR HEAD,
NOD YOUR HEAD.
FIVE, SIX,
MOVE YOUR ARMS,
MOVE YOUR LEGS.
SEVEN, EIGHT,
MOVE YOUR BODY
NINE, TEN,
AND START AGAIN.
MUM IS HAPPY
ONE, TWO, THREE,
YOU SLEEP HAPPILY
ONE, TWO, THREE.

THE DRAGON HAS GOT A COLD
(WINTER AND CLOTHES)

ONCE UPON A TIME THERE WAS A DRAGON. HE SLEPT UPSIDE-DOWN. WHEN HE SLEPT HE REMOVED THE SHEET WITH HIS TAIL: "SHH, SHH, SHH" THE SHEET WENT OUT AND NEXT DAY:
 'ATISHOO!'
HE HAS GOT A COLD. MUM TOOK HIM TO THE DOCTOR. HE GAVE HIM AN INJECTION.

DRAGON, DRAGON
HAS GOT A COLD
ATISHOO!, ATISHOO!
INJECTION, INJECTION,
OH NO, OH NO!

'YOU MUJST WEAR A HEAVY JACKET,' SAID MUM
BUT, AT NIGHT, HE REMOVED HIS SHEET… AND NEXT DAY:
'ATIHOO!'
ANOTHER INJECTION.
'YOU MUST WEAR YOUR SCARF.'
BUT, AT NIGHT, HE REMOVED HIS SHEET… AND NEXT DAY:
'ATIHOO!'
ANOTHER INJECTION.
'YOU MUST WEAR YOUR HEAVY SHOCK AND YOUR HEAVY SHOES.'

JACKET, JACKET
YES, YES, YES
SCARF, SCARF
YES, YES, YES
SOCKS AND SHOES
YES, YES, YES…

JACKET
AND SHOES

SCARF

SOCKS

NEXT DAY…
'ATISHOO!'
'YOU MUST WEAR A HEAVY SWEATER.'
NEXT DAY…
'ATISHOO!'
'YOU MUST WEAR YOUR HEAVY TROUSERS.'
ONE DAY HIS TAIL HURT BECAUSE OF INJECTIONS AND HE DECIDED TO SLEEP ON HIS SIDE. HIS TAIL DIDN'T MOVE AT NIGHT.

SWEATER, SWEATER
YES, YES, YES
TROUSERS, TROUSERS
YES, YES, YES
OH NO MY TAIL!
OH NO, OH NO!

NEXT DAY HE WASN'T SICK.
'DRAGONS CAN'T SLEEP UPSIDE-DOWN', SAID THE BOY.
'BUT IT'S IMPORTANT TO SLEEP WELL AT NIGHT…
'GOOD NIGHT,' SAID MUM.
'GOOD NIGHT,' SAID THE BOY.
HE FELL ASLEEP.

SLEEP WELL

YES, YES, YES

YOU AREN'T SICK

ONE, TWO, THREE.

SLEEP WELL

DRAGON, DRAGON
HAS GOT A COLD
ATISHOO!, ATISHOO!
INJECTION, INJECTION,
OH NO, OH NO!
JACKET, JACKET
YES, YES, YES
SCARF, SCARF
YES, YES, YES
SOCKS AND SHOES
YES, YES, YES
SWEATER, SWEATER
YES, YES, YES
TROUSERS, TROUSERS
YES, YES, YES
OH NO MY TAIL!
OH NO, OH NO!
SLEEP WELL
YES, YES, YES
YOU AREN'T SICK
ONE, TWO, THREE.

LET'S GO TO THE RESTAURANT
(FOOD)

IT WAS MUM'S BIRTHDAY. MUM, DAD, THE BROTHER AND HIS SISTER WENT TO THE RESTAURANT TO HAVE DINNER. CHILDREN LIKED GOING TO THE RESTAU-RANT. 'WHAT DO YOU WANT?' SAID THE WAITER.

HAPPY FAMILY, HAPPY FAMILY,
MUM, DAD, BROTHER AND SISTER
GO TO THE RESTAURANT.
WHAT DO YOU WANT?

FAMILY

WAITER

MUM

DAD

BROTHER

SISTER

'I WANT A BURGER, EGG AND CHIPS, PLEASE,' SAID THE BROTHER.
'I WANT SOME MEAT WITH LOTS OF PEAS, PLEASE,' SAID THE SISTER.
'I WANT FISH AND CHIPS, PLEASE,' SAID MUM.
'I WANT SPAGHETTI, PLEASE' SAID DAD.

WHAT DO YOU WANT?
BURGER, EGG AND CHIPS,
MEAT, CHIPS AND PEAS,
FISH AND CHIPS,
SPAGHETTI, PLEASE.

BURGER, EGG AND CHIPS   MEAT, CHIPS AND PEAS

FISH AND CHIPS   SPAGHETTI

'DO YOU WANT SOMETHING TO DRINK?'
'WINE, COKE, JUICE AND WATER, PLEASE,' SAID MUM.
DO YOU WANT ICE CREAM?' ASKED THE WAITER.
'YES, I DO,' SAID THE BROTHER, 'CHOCOLATE ICE CREAM, PLEASE.'
'I WANT SOME FRUIT, PLEASE,' SAID THE SISTER.'
'COFFEE, PLEASE,' SAID MUM.
'TEA, PLEASE,' SAID DAD.

WINE, COKE, JUICE
AND WATER, PLEASE.
ICE CREAM AND FRUIT
COFFEE AND TEA.

ICE CREAM   FRUIT

COFFEE   TEA

FINALLY THE BROTHER AND HIS SISTER WENT TO THE CHILDREN'S GAME AREA WHILE MUM AND DAD RELAXED.
THEY WENT HOME BY CAR. THE BROTHER AND HIS SISTER WERE TIRED AND THEY FELL ASLEEP.
IT WAS A NICE DAY.

PLAY, PLAY, PLAY
YES, YES, YES
GO BY CAR
YES, YES, YES,
WE ARE HAPPY
ONE, TWO, THREE.

THE RESTAURANT

HAPPY FAMILY, HAPPY FAMILY
MUM, DAD, BROTHER AND SISTER
GO TO THE RESTAURANT.
WHAT DO YOU WANT?
BURGER, EGG AND CHIPS,
MEAT, CHIPS AND PEAS,
FISH AND CHIPS,
SPAGHETTI, PLEASE.
WINE, COKE, JUICE
AND WATER, PLEASE.
ICE CREAM AND FRUIT
COFFEE AND TEA.
PLAY, PLAY, PLAY
YES, YES, YES
GO BY CAR
YES, YES, YES,
WE ARE HAPPY
ONE, TWO, THREE.

HENS SHARE EASTER EGGS
(SPRING, PLANTS AND EASTER)

ONCE UPON A TIME THERE WAS A VERY HAPPY HEN. SHE HAS GOT LOTS OF FRIENDS. SHE LAID LOTS OF EGGS.
THERE WAS ANOTHER HEN. SHE WAS SAD. SHE DIDN'T HAVE FRIENDS. SHE COULDN'T LAY EGGS.

HAPPY HEN, HAPPY HEN
EGGS, EGGS, EGGS,
SAD HEN, SAD HEN
NO, NO, NO.

ONE DAY THE HAPPY HEN WANTED TO PLAY.
'DO YOU WANT TO COME AND PLAY?'
'I CAN'T'
'WHY?'
'IT'S EASTER DAY. EVERYBODY HAS GOT AN EGG TO PAINT BUT I HAVEN'T GOT ANY EGG,' SAID THE SAD HEN.
'HERE YOU ARE,' SAID THE HAPPY HEN, 'ONE EGG FOR YOU.'
'NOW LE'S GO AND PAINT EASTER EGGS.'

PLAY TOGETHER, PLAY TOGETHER
YES, YES, YES
SHARE EGGS, SHARE EGGS
YES, YES, YES.

THE HENS PAINTED AND PAINTED EASTER EGGS. THEY WERE HAPPY PLAYING TOGETHER. THEY HAD GOT LOTS OF FRIENDS.
«ARE YOU HAPPY?» «THEN, PAINT EASTER EGGS...»
«HAPPY EASTER.»

PAINT EGGS, PAINT EGGS,
ONE, TWO, THREE,
HAPPY EASTER, HAPPY EASTER
FOR YOU AND ME.

HAPPY EASTER

HAPPY HEN, HAPPY HEN
EGGS, EGGS, EGGS,
SAD HEN, SAD HEN
NO, NO, NO.
HERE YOU ARE!
PLAY TOGETHER, PLAY TOGETHER
YES, YES, YES
SHARE EGGS, SHARE EGGS
YES, YES, YES.
PAINT EGGS, PAINT EGGS,
ONE, TWO, THREE,
HAPPY EASTER, HAPPY EASTER
FOR YOU AND ME.

A VERY NAUGHTY SNAKE
(ANIMALS)

ONCE UPON A TIME THERE WAS NICE DIMETRODON. EACH MORNING HE LAY IN THE SUN AND FISHED SOMETHING TO EAT.

THAT MORNING THERE WAS A SNAKE WATCHING HIM. THE SNAKE WENT TO THE WATER. SHE SMILED.

'I'M HUNGRY. A FISH, PLEASE.

'OK. HERE YOU ARE,' SAID THE DIMETRODON AND HE GAVE HER A FISH.

DIMETRODON, DIMETRODON
HAPPY, HAPPY, HAPPY,
SNAKE, SNAKE,
HUNGRY, HUNGRY, HUNGRY.

THE SNAKE ATE IT "YUM, YUM, YUM!", BUT SHE WAS VERY HUNGRY.
'PLEASE, ANOTHER ONE.'
'BUT… THAT'S ALL.'
THE DIMETRODON GAVE HER OTHER FISH. THE SNAKE ATE IT "YUM, YUM, YUM!" BUT THE SNAKE WAS HUNGRY.
'A FISH, PLEASE.'
'NO, NO, NO… GO AWAY.
SNAKE WENT ON LOOKING AT THE WATER AGAIN. A MOSASAURUS WAS EATING A BIG FISH "YUM, YUM, YUM!"

A FISH, PLEASE,
YES, YES, YES
ANOTHER FISH
NO, NO, NO.,,

THE SNAKE WAS HUNGRY… SHE SMILED AT HIM:
'I'M HUNGRY. A FISH, PLEASE.'
'JUST ONE AND GO AWAY.'
'OK,' SAID THE SNAKE.
THE MOSASAURUS GAVE HER A SMALL FISH, BUT THE SNAKE
WAS VERY HUNGRY.
'ANOTHER ONE, PLEASE.'
'NO, NO, NO… GO AWAY.'
SNAKE WENT ON LOOKING AT THE WATER.

MOSASAURUS,
BIG, BIG, BIG
SNAKE, SNAKE,
HUNGRY, HUNGRY.
A FISH, PLEASE,
YES, YES, YES
ANOTHER ONE
NO, NO, NO.

A GIANT TYRANNOSAURUS WAS EATING WITH HIS ENORMOUS TEETH…
THE SNAKE SMILED. THE TYRANNOSAURUS SMILED TOO. HE LOOKED AT HER, AND OPENED HIS MOUTH AND… HE SAID:
'GO AWAY AND WORK.'
SNAKE GOES AWAY QUICKLY.
'OK, OK. I'M GOING TO WORK'
'GOOD IDEA!'

TYRANNOSAURUS,

BIG TEETH, BIG TEETH,

SNAKE, SNAKE, SNAKE,

WORK, WORK, WORK,

AND YUM, YUM, YUM!

ANIMALS

DIMETRODON
HAPPY, HAPPY, HAPPY,
SNAKE, SNAKE,
HUNGRY, HUNGRY, HUNGRY.
A FISH, PLEASE,
YES, YES, YES
ANOTHER ONE
NO, NO, NO.
MOSASAURUS,
BIG, BIG, BIG
SNAKE, SNAKE,
HUNGRY, HUNGRY.
A FISH, PLEASE,
YES, YES, YES
ANOTHER ONE
NO, NO, NO.
TYRANNOSAURUS,
BIG TEETH, BIG TEETH,
SNAKE, SNAKE, SNAKE,
WORK, WORK, WORK,
AND YUM, YUM, YUM!

I WANT AN ICE CREAM
(SUMMER)

IN SUMMER CHILDREN LIKE ICE CREAMS: STRAWBERRY, BANANA, CHOCOLATE, PINEAPPLE ICE CREAMS…
'WHAT ICE CREAM DO YOU LIKE? ASKED MUM.
'I WANT A CHOCOLATE ICE CREAM, PLEASE,' SAID THE SMALL BOY ONE DAY.
ANOTHER DAY:
'A CHOCOLATE ICE CREAM, PLEASE…'
THE SAME HAPPENED ALL THE SUMMER.

ICE CREAM IN SUMMER
YES, YES, YES,
CHOCOLATE ICE CREAM
PLEASE, PLEASE.

ICE CREAMS

BUT A COLD DAY IN SEPTEMBER THE SMALL BOY WANTED AN ICE CREAM. HE WENT TO MUM:
'CAN I HAVE A CHOCOLATE ICE CREAM, MUM, PLEASE...?'
'NO, YOU CAN'T.'
HE WENT TO DAD:
'AN ICE CREAM, PLEASE, DAD...'
'NO, IT'S TOO COLD.'
HE WENT TO GRANDAD:
'ICE CREAM, PLEASE.'
'NO, NO, NO...'
HE WENT TO GRANNY:
'AN ICE CREAM, PLEASE, PLEASE...'
'OK, BUT...'

ICE CREAM IN WINTER
NO, NO, NO,
ICE CREAM, DAD
NO, NO, NO.
ICE CREAM, MUM
NO, NO, NO
ICE CREAM, GRANDAD
NO, NO, NO
ICE CREAM, GRANNY
YES, BUT....

DAD   MUM   GRANDAD   GRANNY   BROTHER

THE NEXT DAY THE SMALL BOY WAS SICK. HE COULDN'T EAT ANYTHING. HE HAD GOT A TERRIBLE SORE THROAT AND A HEADACHE… HE SAID:
'NO ICE CREAM, NO ICE CREAM… IT'S TOO COLD.'
'OK,' SAID MUM. 'YOU MUSTN'T EAT ICE CREAMS WHEN IT'S COLD, OK?
TWO DAYS LATER HE WAS HEALTHY, BUY HE DIDN'T ASK FOR ICE CREAMS.

A COLD, A COLD, A COLD

OH NO, OH NO!

NO ICE CREAMS IN WINTER

ONE, TWO, THREE.

ICE CREAM

ICE CREAM IN SUMMER
YES, YES, YES,
CHOCOLATE ICE CREAM
PLEASE, PLEASE.
ICE CREAM IN WINTER
NO, NO, NO,
ICE CREAM , DAD
NO, NO, NO.
ICE CREAM, MUM
NO,NO, NO
ICE CREAM GRANDAD
NO, NO, NO
ICE CREAM, GRANNY
YES, BUT….
A COLD, A COLD, A COLD
OH NO, OH NO!
NO ICE CREAMS IN WINTER
ONE, TWO, THREE.

A TREE WITHOUT NAME
(EARTH DAY / "DÍA DEL ÁRBOL")

ONCE UPON A TIME THERE WAS A TREE. IT HASN'T GOT A NAME BECAUSE IT IS NOT PAINTED. AN ANT ARRIVES THERE.
'WHAT'S YOUR NAME?
I HAVEN'T GOT A NAME. CAN YOU PAINT ME?' SAYS THE TREE.
'YES, YOU CAN BE AN APPLE TREE,' SAYS THE ANT.
THE ANT PAINTS LOTS OF SPOTS AND GREEN LEAVES. BUT SHE GETS BORED AND SHE GOES AWAY TO PLAY.

WHAT'S YOUR NAME?
WHAT'S YOUR NAME?
APPLE TREE, APPLE TREE
ANT SAYS NO, NO, NO...

DOG ARRIVES THERE. HE GOES ON PAINTING IT.
'CAN YOU PAINT ME?'
'YES, YOU CAN BE A CHERRY TREE. I LIKE CHERRIES. DO YOU?'
BUT THE DOG'S MUM CALLED HIM TO HAVE A SANDWICH AND HE GOES AWAY.

WHAT'S YOUR NAME?
WHAT'S YOUR NAME?
CHERRY TREE, CHERRY TREE
DOG SAYS NO, NO, NO…

A BULL ARRIVES THERE. HE TRIES TO PAINT THE TREE.
'CAN YOU PAINT ME?'
'YES, YOU CAN BE A PEAR TREE. I EAT LOTS OF PEARS
EVERY DAY...'
SUDDENLY THE BULL WANTS TU RUN. HE RUNS AND RUNS
AND HE GOES AWAY.

WHAT'S YOUR NAME?
WHAT'S YOUR NAME?
PEAR TREE, PEAR TREE
BULL SAYS NO, NO, NO...

THERE IS A RESPONSIBLE CHILD LIKE YOU. HE HAS FINISHED HIS HOMEWORK, HE HAS HAD HIS AFTERNOON SANDWICH AND HI LIKES PAINTING.
'CAN YOU PAINT ME?'
'YES, I CAN.'
HE FINISHES PAINTING IT. IT IS AN ORANGE TREE.
'THANK YOU.'
'YOU ARE WELCOME!'
AFTER THAT THE TREE HAS GOT A NAME FOR EVER BECAUSE THE CHILD IS RESPONSIBLE AND HAS FINISHED HIS WORK.

WHAT'S YOUR NAME?
WHAT'S YOUR NAME?
ORANGE TREE, ORANGE TREE
YOU SAY YES, YES, YES…

WHAT'S YOUR NAME?
ORANGE TREE, ORANGE TREE
YOU ARE HAPPY
ONE, TWO, THREE….

TREE

WHAT'S YOUR NAME?
WHAT'S YOUR NAME?
APPLE TREE, APPLE TREE
ANT SAYS NO, NO, NO…

WHAT'S YOUR NAME?
WHAT'S YOUR NAME?
CHERRY TREE, CHERRY TREE
DOG SAYS NO, NO, NO…

WHAT'S YOUR NAME?
WHAT'S YOUR NAME?
PEAR TREE, PEAR TREE
BULL SAYS NO, NO, NO…

WHAT'S YOUR NAME?
WHAT'S YOUR NAME?
ORANGE TREE, ORANGE TREE
YOU SAY YES, YES, YES…

WHAT'S YOUR NAME?
ORANGE TREE, ORANGE TREE
YOU ARE HAPPY
ONE, TWO, THREE…

THE SUN AND DE MOON WANTED TO GET MARRIED *(MOTHER'S DAY)*

THE SUN AND THE MOON WANT TO GET MARRIED BUT THEY CAN'T. THE SUN GOES AUT DURING THE DAY AND THE MOON GOES OUT AT NIGHT.

I LOVE YOU
YOU LOVE ME,
THE SUN LOVES
THE MOON,
ONE, TWO, THREE.

A MAGICIAN MAKES MAGIC: 'THICKY, TROKY, WICKY, WICK'
AND GIVES THEM AN OPPORTUNITY TO GET MARRIED: YOU
MUST BE ON YOUR BEST BEHAVIOUR DURING A WHOLE DAY.
YOU HAVE ONLY A WEEK TO GET IT.
ON MONDAY HE DOEN'T PICK UP HIS TOYS AND HIS MOTHER
GETS ANGRY. THEY CAN'T GET MARRIED.

TRICKY, WICKY, WITCH,
TOYS, TOYS,
PICK UP YOUR TOYS.

ON TUESDAY HE DOESN'T BRUSH HIS TEETH AFTER LUNCH. HIS MOTHER GETS ANGRY. THEY CAN'T GET MARRIED.
ON WEDNESDAY HE DOESN'T WANT TO HAVE A SHOWER WHEN HIS MOTHER ASKS HIM. SHE GETS ANGRY. THEY CAN'T GET MARRIED.

TRICKY, WICKY, WITCH,
TEETH, TEETH,
BRUSH YOUR TEETH.

TRICKY, WICKY, WITCH,
SHOWER, SHOWER,
HAVE A SHOWER.

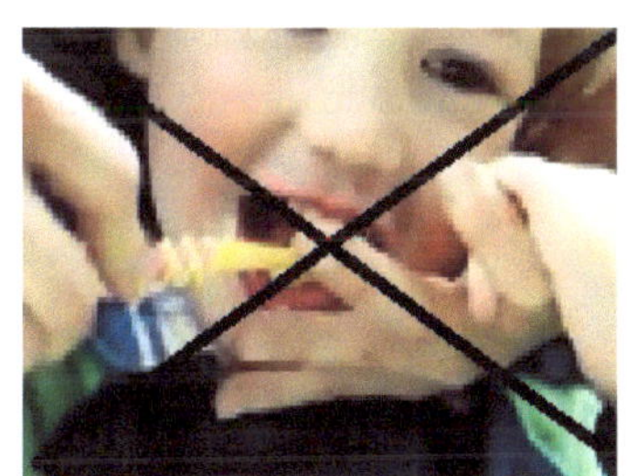
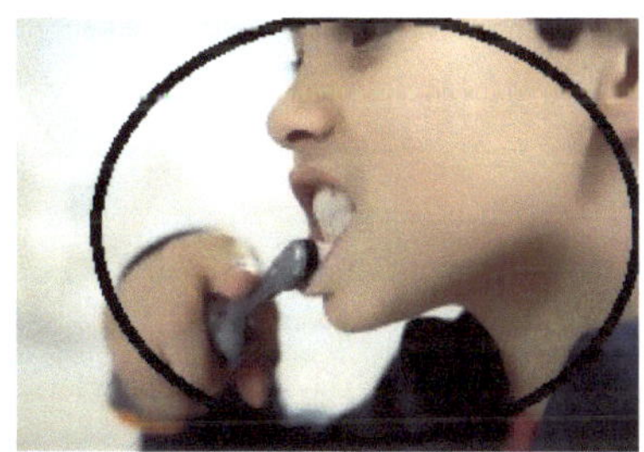

ON THURSDAY HE DOESN'T EAT HIS FOOK. HE PROTESTS. HIS
MOTHER HAS TO HELP HIM. THEY CAN'T GET MARRIED.
ON FRIDAY HE DOESN'T SHARE HIS TOYS WITH A PARTNER.
HIS MOTHER GETS ANGRY. THEY CAN'T GET MARRIED.

TRICKY, WICKY, WITCH,
VEGETABLES, VEGETABLES,
EAT YOUR VEGETABLES.

TRICKY, WICKY, WITCH,
FRIENDS, FRIENDS,
SHARE YOUR TOYS.

ON SATURDAY HE FORGETS TO FLUSH THE TOILET AND TURN OFF THE LIGHT. THEY CAN'T GET MARRIED.

FINALLY, THERE IS ONLY ONE DAY TO BE ON HIS BEST BEHAVIOUR. "CAN YOU GET IT?" "I THINK SO…" "DO YOU PICK UP YOUR TOYS?" "YES? OK" "DO YOU BRUSH YOUR TEETH?" "YES? OK" "DO YOU HAVE A SHOWER?" "YES? OK" "DO YOU EAT VEGETABLES?" "YES? OK" "DO YOU SHARE YOUR TOYS?" "YES? OK" AND "DO YOU FLUSH THE TOILET AND TURN OFF THE LIGHT?" "YES? OK", "ARE YOU SURE?" "YES, OK"

TRICKY, WICKY, WITCH,
TOILET, TOILET,
FLUSH THE TOILET.

TRICKY, WICKY, WITCH,
TOYS, TEETH, SHOWER,
VEGETABLES, TOYS, TOILET.

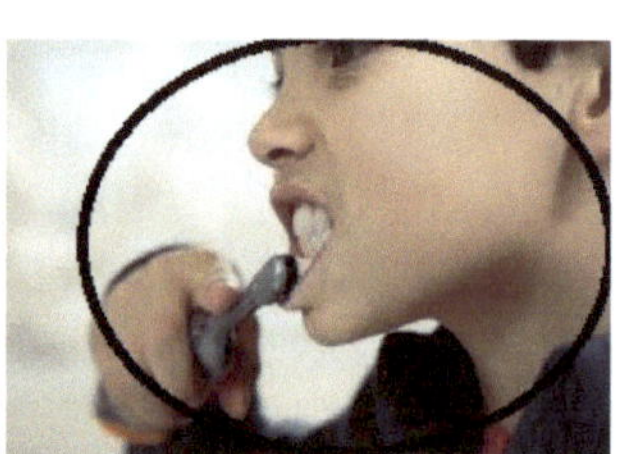

WHEN THE DAY FINISHED HE ASKS HIS MUM: MUM, IS THAT OK? ARE YOU HAPPY?

'YES, IT'S OK. I'M VERY HAPPY.'
FINALLY THE SUN AND THE MOON CAN GET MARRIED.
'MUM, WHAT DO YOU WANT FOR "MOTHER'S DAY?'
'GOOD BEHAVIOUR EVERY DAY'
'HAPPY MOTHER'S DAY.'

I LOVE YOU
YOU LOVE ME
HAPPY MOTHER'S DAY
ONE, TWO, THREE.

I LOVE YOU MUM

HAPPY MOTHER'S DAY

HAPPY MOTHER'S DAY

I LOVE YOU
YOU LOVE ME,
THE SUN LOVES
THE MOON,
ONE, TWO, THREE.
TRICKY, WICKY, WITCH,
TOYS, TOYS,
PICK UP YOUR TOYS.
TRICKY, WICKY, WITCH,
TEETH, TEETH,
BRUSH YOUR TEETH.
TRICKY, WICKY, WITCH,
SHOWER, SHOWER,
HAVE A SHOWER.
TRICKY, WICKY, WITCH,
VEGETABLES, VEGETABLES,
EAT YOUR VEGETABLES.
TRICKY, WICKY, WITCH,
FRIENDS, FRIENDS,
SHARE YOUR TOYS.
TRICKY, WICKY, WITCH,
TOILET , TOILET,
FLUSH THE TOILET.
TRICKY, WICKY, WITCH,
TOYS, TEETH, SHOWER,
VEGETABLES, TOYS, TOILET.
I LOVE YOU
YOU LOVE ME
HAPPY MOTHER'S DAY
ONE, TWO, THREE.

DAD, THERE'S A CHOCOLATE CAKE FOR YOU! *(FATHER'S DAY)*

IT'S HOLIDAY. DAD IS ALL THE TIME AT THE COMPUTER LOOKING FOR INFORMATION ON THE INTERNET. DAD FORGETS MUM AND HIS SMALL CHILD.
MUM AND HER CHILD ARE BORED, VERY BORED, AND THE BOY HAS GOT AN IDEA.
'DAD!' THE GOY SHOUTS OUT. 'THERE IS A CHOCOLATE CAKE FOR YOU!'

MUM, DAD, BROTHER,
MUM, DAD, BROTHER,
THIS IS MY FAMILY.

DAD LEAVES THE COMPUTER. HE RUNS TO THE KITCHEN TO LOOK FOR THE CAKE. HE OPENS THE CUPBOARDS, THE FRIDGE, THE TABLE DRAWERS… HE LOOKS AT MUM AND HIS CHILD. THEY ARE READY TO GO OUT. THEY GO FOR A WALK.

DAD, CHOCOLATE CAKE!
NO, NO, NO.
LET'S GO, LET'S GO…

THE NEXT DAY:
'DAD!' THE CHILD SHOUTS OUT. 'THERE IS A CHOCOLATE CAKE FOR YOU!'
DAD IS VERY BUSY. HE HAS LOTS OF PROGRAMMES ON THE INTERNET THAT HE VANTS TO CLOSE. HE COMES WITH SPORT SHOES. THEY GO SHOPPING.

DAD, CHOCOLATE CAKE!
NO, NO, NO.
LET'S GO, LET'S GO…

THE THIRD DAY MUM AND HER CHILD BUY A SMALL CHOCOLATE CAKE. THE CHILD SHOUTS OUT LUDLY:
'DAD, THERE'S A CHOCOLATE CAKE FOR YOU!'
'NO, NO, NO...,' SAYS DAD. THIS IS IMPORTANT. LATER... I'M BUSY... YOU CAN EAT THE CAKE. EAT THE CAKE FOR ME...
 'ARE YOU SURE?'
'YES, YES, YES. EAT ALL THE CAKE.'
'OK, DAD.'
MUM AND HER CHILD EAT ALL THE CAKE.

MUM, CHOCOLATE CAKE,
YES, YES, YES.
YAM, YAM, YAM...

BROTHER, CHOCOLATE CAKE,
YES, YES, YES
YAM, YAM, YAM.

WHEN DAD SEES THE RESTS OF THE FOOD HE REGRETS IT. HE THIKS: "NEXT TIME I MUST PAY MORTE ATTENTION TO MY FAMILY…"

DAD CHANGES. HE IS HAPPY WITH HIS FAMILY. HE PLAYS WITH HIS CHILD. FOR FATHER'S DAY, DAD HAS GOT A PRESENT: A BIG CHOCOLATE CAKE.

YOU ARE MY DAD,
I LOVE YOU
YOU LOVE ME
HAPPY FATHER'S DAY
ONE, TWO, THREE.

FATHER'S DAY

MUM, DAD, BROTHER,
MUM, DAD, BROTHER,
THIS IS MY FAMILY.
DAD, CHOCOLATE CAKE!
NO, NO, NO.
LET'S GO, LET'S GO…
MUM, CHOCOLATE CAKE,
YES, YES, YES.
YAM, YAM, YAM…
BROTHER, CHOCOLATE CAKE,
YES, YES, YES
YAM, YAM, YAM.
YOU ARE MY DAD,
I LOVE YOU
YOU LOVE ME
HAPPY FATHER'S DAY
ONE, TWO, THREE.